Wagstaff, Sue
Wayne is adopted.
1. Adoption – Great Britain
I. Title
362.7'34'0941   HV875
ISBN 0-7136-2141-9

Acknowledgments

The author, photographer and publishers would like to thank the King family without whose help and co-operation this book would not have been possible; the staff and pupils of Wayne's school; Margaret Mawr of the British Agencies for Adoption and Fostering; Madeleine Blakeley of the National Association for Multi-Racial Education.

For permission to use copyright material, Bucks and Herts Newspapers Ltd.

A & C Black (Publishers) Limited
35 Bedford Row, London WC1R 4JH

ISBN 0-7136-2141-9

© A & C Black (Publishers) Limited

All rights reserved. No part of this publication may be reproduced, stored in a retrieval system, or transmitted, in any form or by any means, electronic, mechanical, photocopying, recording or otherwise, without the prior permission of A & C Black (Publishers) Limited.

Filmset by August Filmsetting, Reddish, Stockport.
Printed in Hong Kong by Dai Nippon.

Wayne is Adopted

Sue Wagstaff
Photographs by Chris Fairclough

Adam & Charles Black · London

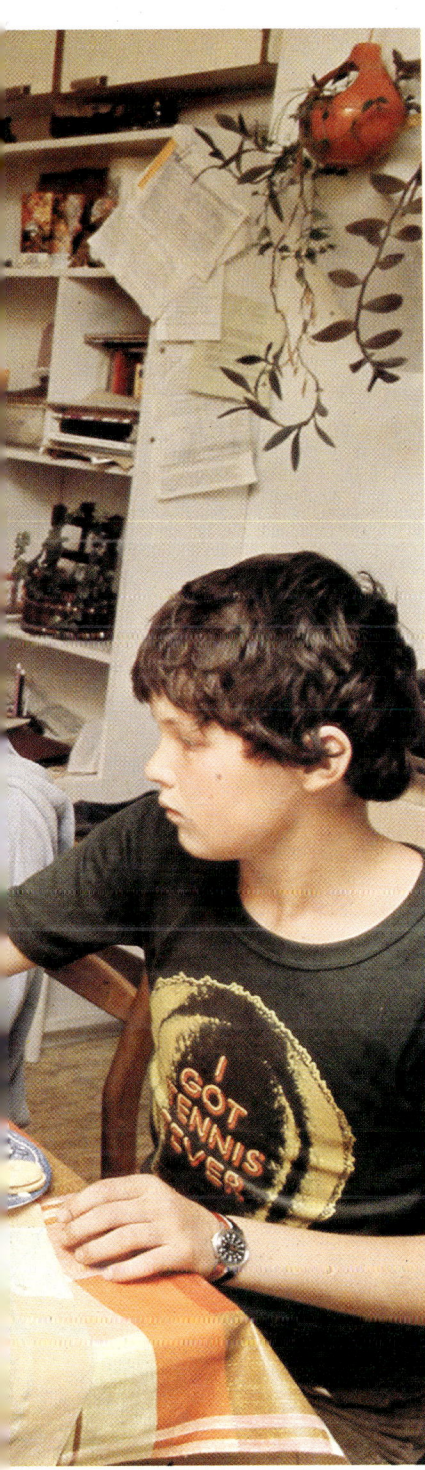

This is the King family.
There are five children in the family; Paul, Nigel, Emma, Wayne and Rachel.
Wayne and Emma are adopted.

Emma was adopted when she was a baby.
Wayne was adopted when he was eight years old.

Adoption means that grown-ups become parents to children they did not give birth to. Adopted children become members of a family just like any other children. They belong to their adopted family for ever.

Wayne's first mum was black.
His first dad was white.
They weren't married.

It was difficult for Wayne's mum to look after him by herself, so, when he was five days old, Wayne went to stay with foster parents. They were going to care for Wayne until his mum could look after him properly. Wayne's mum paid the foster parents to do this.

But Wayne's mum went away and his foster parents couldn't afford to look after him any more. So Wayne went to live in a children's home. He was only a few months old.

Wayne liked the children's home.
He says 'It was big and you had lots of friends to play with. There was a big garden. I liked living with all the children. They were all about my age so I didn't have to worry about getting on with them. We rode in barrels down a big hill. We climbed trees, put a rope on a tree and swung on it. And we played games indoors.'

Before he was adopted, Wayne lived in two children's homes and stayed with three foster families (people who had Wayne to live with them for a time, but who did not adopt him).

When Mr and Mrs King decided they might like to adopt Wayne, they went to meet him at the children's home. Later on, they took all their children to meet him, too. After that, Wayne went to stay with the family for afternoons, weekends and at half-term holidays.

Wayne knows all about this because his new mum and dad helped him make a book about his life. Wayne has photographs of the children's homes, his friends and his adoptive family in his book.

Mr and Mrs King wanted to adopt an older child. In the past, not many families adopted older children, but more and more do now.

Mrs King says 'When we first heard about Wayne, we wondered if he would like to join our family and if he would like us. It was a family decision to adopt Wayne. We wanted to share our family life with a child who had no home of his own.'

'We wanted to adopt a black child. We felt that a black child could easily find a place in our family because Emma is black too. Emma didn't mind if we adopted a boy or a girl. But the boys said it had to be a boy!'

Emma says 'First of all mum and dad asked us if we wanted a boy or a girl. I had to move into a bedroom with my sister. Wayne had my bedroom. I wasn't too pleased about it at first, but I got used to it.'

'I was worried Wayne might be different from us. It took about six months and then he was part of the family. I don't spend much time with him really. He boasts a bit about how good he is at sport, but he makes me laugh too.'

Paul says 'I didn't mind Wayne coming here. I might have felt differently if he had been older than me though. It didn't make any difference to me that he was black. Why should it? I spend quite a lot of time with him. We play football a lot.'

Wayne was adopted on 12 May 1978. All the family went to court. Wayne can't remember much about it except that the courtroom was dark and gloomy.

Mr King says 'It was all over in five minutes. The judge came in. We filled up the front bench. The judge looked down at Wayne and said "Do you know what it means to be adopted?" I nudged Wayne to say something so he said "Yes"! The judge said he hoped Wayne would be happy. That was it! We celebrated with a big family meal at a restaurant.'

Wayne says 'I was a bit sad when I left the children's home. I liked it there. I was worried about getting on with the other children in my family. But I'm happy now.'

The Bucks Herald

Established 1832   Thursday, 18th May, 1978   Price 6p

ADOPTION

KING. — Philip and Audrey, adopted Wayne Brian on May 12th. God bless you son.

Wayne and Rachel go to the same primary school. Mrs King works there as a dinner lady. The other children go to the local comprehensive school.

Mrs King says 'Wayne isn't teased much at school. He gets on well with the children and the teachers. He can always find someone to play with. But we are aware that Wayne may face some problems when he gets older. It might be difficult for him to get a job because he's black and some people may pick on him.'

At school, Wayne likes history and writing stories. But, best of all, he likes games and PE, especially football. He plays centre-forward in the school football team and also plays in a five-a-side team. He usually wins lots of events at the annual school sports day.

Wayne is also in the Cubs. He is a sixer, in charge of Red group. At the moment, Wayne is doing his link badge so that he can become a scout. He goes to scout meetings on Mondays and cub meetings on Thursdays. After six weeks, he will become a scout.

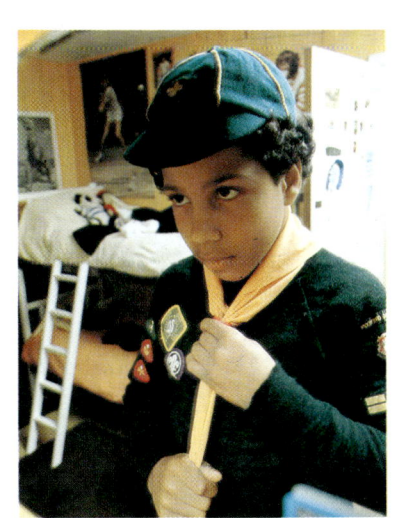

At pack meetings, the cubs sing, play games, make models, tie knots and do map work. There is an annual sports day when all the local cub packs compete. Wayne wins a lot of events then, too!

At the weekends, Wayne often watches TV. He likes Match of the Day and the films. Sometimes he plays with his friends over in the recreation ground. They play football, ride their bicycles or try to knock conkers down from the trees!

All the children have a few jobs to do around the house, like cleaning shoes and making the beds. They each have one day a week when they do the washing up. On Sundays, everybody helps. Wayne helps his mum to keep his bedroom tidy.

There are arguments in the King family, just like any family, but most of the time everyone gets on well together.

Wayne says 'I have arguments with my brothers and sisters. If I annoy Rachel, she shouts at me and sometimes pulls my hair. Emma teases me. I'm always having fights with Nigel because I call him names. My mum comes and sorts it out. I like having lots of brothers and sisters – there's always someone to play with.'

Every year, in the summer, the family goes camping in Sussex. They go with another family. They camp in a big field, a long way from anywhere. It is very quiet and beautiful. Wayne likes going on holiday. *He says* 'It's really great! We do all sorts of things – go to amusement arcades, down to the beach, play tennis, go swimming and visit places.'

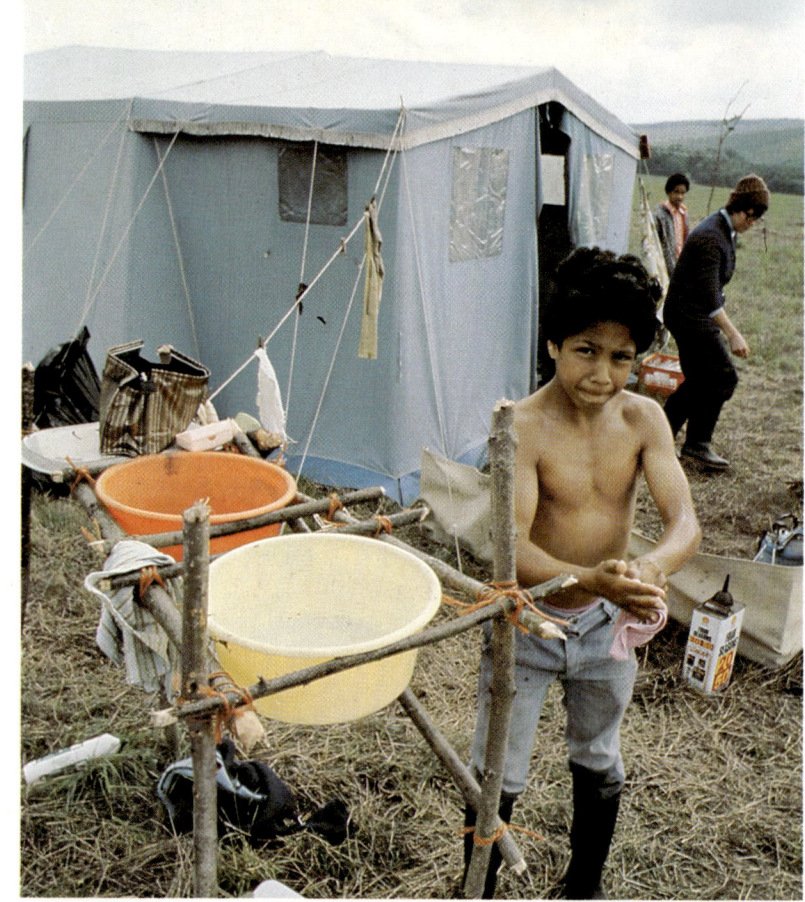

All the children help their parents at the camp. They help to cook breakfast, prepare the picnics and collect wood for the evening campfire. The families usually go out for the day and return to the camp around 7 o'clock. In the evenings, they sit around the campfire and chat or play volleyball.

Today is Wayne's birthday. He is eleven years old. It is a family tradition that the person whose birthday it is, can decide between a birthday party or an outing. This year, Wayne has chosen to go to an Arsenal football match. Wayne supports Arsenal and has already been to see them twice. He has an Arsenal scarf and a sports bag.

Arsenal are playing at home so Wayne has to travel to London for the match. His dad and his friend, Johnny, go with him.

Mr and Mrs King have told Wayne and Emma about their first parents.

Mrs King says 'I think it's important for Wayne and Emma to know about their parents and the countries they came from. It sounds nice in theory, but it's sometimes difficult to explain. Wayne and Emma's parents come from such a mixture of backgrounds and countries – Asia, Africa, Europe and the Caribbean. Which countries do we talk to them about? Each one has its own traditions and history.'

'We've had world maps out showing where their parents came from and where they travelled. When a programme about different parts of the world is on the television, we always try to watch it. Wayne has relatives in the Caribbean and he might want to go there one day.'

'The biggest and most difficult thing is to be fair to all the children – just like in any family. When he first came, Wayne did need more attention. The other children understood this at first but after six months, as far as they were concerned, he'd been with us for ages.'

'Wayne gets fed up at times. He can get upset if he loses a game or gets told off. But he soon gets over it and is getting less touchy all the time. We're all really pleased he joined our family.'

And how does Wayne feel about being adopted?
'Not much really,' he says. 'It's all right and I'm happy.'

Some more books to read

CROMPTON, M. *The house where Jack lives*. Bodley Head
KORNITZER, M. *Mr Fairweather and his family*. Bodley Head
KORNITZER, M. *The Hollywell Family*. Bodley Head
LAPSLEY, S. *I am adopted*. Bodley Head

A full list of adoption and fostering pamphlets for parents is available on request from BAAF, 11 Southwark Street, London SE1 1RQ.

Some useful addresses

British Agencies for Adoption and Fostering (BAAF)
11 Southwark Street,
London SE1 1RQ

Child Welfare League of America
67 Irving Place
New York 10003

Parent to Parent Information on Adoption Services (PPIAS)
26 Belsize Grove,
London NW3

National Association for Multi-Racial Education (NAME)
23 Doles Lane,
Findern, Derby DE6 6AX

Centre for Urban and Educational Studies (CUES)
34 Aberdeen Park
London N5 2BL
(useful for lists of books suited to the multi-racial society)

Federation of New Zealand Parents Centres Inc.
PO Box 11-310
Wellington
New Zealand